Psalms

of the

New Testament

BETH MARIE HAWLEY

ISBN 979-8-88751-379-9 (paperback)
ISBN 979-8-88751-380-5 (digital)

Christian Faith Publishing
832 Park Avenue
Meadville, PA 16335
www.christianfaithpublishing.com

Printed in the United States of America

For my Lord Jesus to honor His greatest gift of salvation. To honor my children, Thane Richard and Amy Marie, my two greatest blessings. Loving them has given me greater insight to the enormity of the love of Jesus.

New Testament Psalms

I have always loved the book of Psalms. The musicality of some, as well as the praise aspect, drew me to them at a young age. I want to give the praise Jesus deserves as the Father received in the early Psalms.

I do not have David's capacity for writing, but I do have the love needed to try. I would never compare myself to the great King David or other great men who wrote the Psalms. This is simply my tribute to Jesus.

I have always enjoyed bringing to attention the story and glory of the Lord Jesus. He has been the greatest historical figure of all time. The sacrifice Jesus made cannot be repeated.

The magnitude of His suffering, physically, emotionally, and spiritually is beyond all human understanding. The dichotomy of His identity, having been fully God and fully man must be recognized and acknowledged.

The other aspect that needs to be addressed is the fact of Jesus being a part of the Holy Trinity. From what we learn from scripture, the Holy Trinity, three functioning as One God, has always been the reality of God. The Father, the Son, and the Holy Spirit are one in their existence.

The one time they were separated, that we know of, was when Jesus was on the cross. He was asking why He had been forsaken. Jesus accepted His fate and knew the sacrifice He would make. We however, do not give it the significance it deserves.

Knowing Jesus was returned to the Father does not negate the suffering endured during separation. As humans, we will never be able to fully comprehend the existence of three functioning as One God. If we simply acknowledge the fact it exists, we then must be cognizant of the consequences of being separated for even a moment in time. The time separated can only be speculated not known. God does not reveal all to us in this realm. Only God can see all in both realms. As we acknowledge the complexity of our God, we then can appreciate more fully the price Jesus paid.

The Lord has led me to do this writing to bring more appreciation to the prophecy fulfilled that was prophesied in the Psalms of the Old Testament and secondly to acknowledge the complexity of the sacrifice made, as well as our relationship and responsibility related to that sacrifice.

My wish for you is that if even one Psalm brings you closer to our Lord, my calling will be fulfilled. The New Testament Psalms are my dedication to the One I call Savior.

1. How can I walk this life without Your grace, mercy, and
   faithfulness?
   So grateful I don't have to know loneliness or concern.
   You have walked with me through triumph and regret, through
   sorrow and joy.
   My doubts You remove when difficult choices are made.
   Your support and encouragement, always present.
   Never do You allow me to dwell in my own concerns longer
   than You see fit.
   You lift me out of my darkness and encourage my walk to
   enlightenment.
   I know I have never been alone and my future is secure in that
   knowledge.
   I beg You to make a path leading to Your Son for all those who
   have walked away.
   Once they're yours my faith is in Your faithfulness, mercy,
   grace, and love.
   My trust is in the strength of Your commitment to keep Your
   children close.
   My faith is in how You heal pain and loss knowing we cannot
   navigate this world without Your strength and guidance.
   Open their eyes to Your answers, as You opened mine during
   so much loss and heartache.
   Never once was I forsaken in my time of need.
   You spoke to me when all came crashing down and lifted me
   into Your light.

You reassured me of my husband's salvation in Your whispered
words.
Never left with the overwhelming grief that comes with the
loss of the one You chose for me.
Always in my weakness, You have reminded me of the love we
shared.
So young to be left behind, yet You never let me feel lost.
So much comfort when illness took over my life.
You drew me near to become more Your child.
You never let us sink into despair when our hearts are known
to be Yours.
So grateful, so comforted by Your character that never changes.
You're always my strength, my hope, my reassurance to all life's
trials and my comfort in all questions I ask, when only
You know the answers.
My loving Father, my precious Jesus, ever present Holy Spirit,
You carried me when I wasn't aware.
Your strength kept me on the path You carved for me.
Your faithfulness always led me home.
Now I wait for Your next challenge, Your next gift of guidance
and the continued peace that comes from being Your
child.

2.   This world, trapped in the disease of anger.
Lost is the priority of self-sacrifice and the placement of others
over self.
You, our Lord, are the only hope in darkness, the security of
strength in weakness, the reassurance of a kinder path
to walk.
Never can we feel lost, with You by our side.
Help us in our weakness of character to bring You closer.
Give us Your strength of commitment to encourage our growth
in character.
Lift us out of our fear, and remove the plague that not only
affects our bodies but our souls.

You are our only hope in a time of overwhelming loss and in
continued waves of disease and social deterioration.
You are our strength over all politics.
You, Lord, are the light that guides our hope and faith.
Only You, Lord, know the path that will lead us out of
darkness.
Only You, Lord, know the trials that will challenge that path.
We can find comfort in Your character.
We can find comfort in knowing Your character never changes.
Save us from our human weaknesses.
Save us from our wavering faith when all feels lost.
I trust in all Your wisdom and goodness.
I trust You will not let us forget that wisdom and goodness.
Help me to remind others of Your goodness.
Help me to remind others to seek Your wisdom.
My life will be successful with Your guidance.
Always will I trust You in the darkness and have faith in Your
light.

3.   The mountains loom ahead.
The forest dark and deep.
The desert dry and foreboding.
The swamp full of danger and peril.
The plains level and inviting.
The fields green and fertile.
The lakes teaming with life.
The orchard bringing forth fruit.
You, Lord, are the master of it all.
You alone can ease the journey.
You alone can make our path straight.

4.   Grateful I am, Lord, for You are always listening when I cry
out.
Grateful I am, Lord, for You hear my praise.
How can I know my path if I don't listen?
How can You know my devotion without praise?

Please keep me on the path to righteousness.
Please open my eyes to injustice and the needs of others.
Guide me with Your wisdom.
Guide me with Your light and goodness.
Faithful is Your way and Your character.
Faithful You are to those who follow You.
Hopeful is the heart that knows You.
Hopeful I am because of You.
You bring life that is everlasting.
You give enduring faith to those who follow You.
Forever, I will follow You.
Forever, I will share Your Word.

5. The ice lays heavy on the old pine tree. The smaller flexible limbs bend without breaking. The large brittle limbs break under the weight. Don't harden your heart, for it will become brittle under the load. Guard your heart and sway with the Lord's guidance, not the influence of the world. For the world is hard, becoming brittle in time. It collapses under the weight of sin. Guard your heart and leave it only open to the Lord. For He will control the wind and ice to protect you from the weight of the world.

6. We live under the misconception that freedom is being able to do what we want. You, God, tell us freedom is being obedient to You. In doing so, we will use our freedom of choice wisely and for the good of all concerned. Our focus will be less on self and more on You, God.

Your character guides us with love, hope, and trust to follow You obediently. We stumble when we think we make better choices without consulting You. We are deceiving ourselves because our choices reflect the way of the world and not You, Lord. The ways of the world continue to be influenced by evil. We know You, Lord, are never influenced by evil.

You make it very clear, Jesus, that You have power over evil. By not trusting Your guidance, we often follow misguided paths being led for evil gain. Our freedom of choice, without Your guidance, becomes our downfall. Our wants become influenced by the world. We confuse our wants with our needs. You established our needs at creation. Those needs do not change with each generation born. Give us the strength to exercise our freedoms with Your patient, loving, faithful guidance. Our obedience to You will give us freedom.

7.   My legs weak from the journey.
My heart weary from loss and pain.
You are my strength to keep walking.
You are comfort in loss, and relief in pain.
My eyes with tears of watching injustice.
My shoulders heavy from the burden of the suffering of others.
You dry tears and bring justice in *Your* time.
You are strong carrying weary hearts and souls.
My soul is only Yours, Lord, for redeeming and keeping.

8.   Our journey does not need to be alone, we are free to ask for the Lord's guidance.
He comes at the call of your heart or the whisper of your voice.
You can cry out with hands raised or ask in a silent kneel.
It will be answered with presence near and a path set before you.
The path will be straight and true, success coming from Your guidance Lord.
Even when we falter and stumble You remain at our side.
Peace will remain deep in our hearts, and our hope enhanced by grace.
Gratitude and praise is all we need to give in return.
The price was paid, the freedom is ours.

9.   Lord, why do You allow such unrest? Do You think we are capable of peace and love? We know Your love and Your faithfulness. We know how to love as individuals, but how far can we reach out with that love? Will we be able to move beyond

our own four walls? Can we take it beyond our cities, our borders, our country? Our hearts must move beyond the chest to the soul. Our minds must open and allow tolerance to take up residence. Our bodies must go assist others with outstretched arms. Only You, Lord, can sustain us through such trials. You are our only hope, salvation, and peace. You said You will return. You, Jesus, will defeat evil and make all right in the world.

10.   The wind will blow and the rains will come. Times will be hard, and challenges will march on. We can lift each other up, lessening the burden of all. Can we leave each other in the wind watching each blow to and fro? I choose the caring touch when we shelter each other from the rain. I choose kindness to walk along side and be the break for the wind. My heart will break in the wind if not used as a brace. My soul will melt in the rain if not used to protect my neighbor. Give me strength to guide the way for others to find their place. Whether shelter or brace, we can all take a stand. The love from such kindness will then begin to flow. Then maybe we can see what God meant us to be.

11.   Teach me, Lord Jesus, all Your ways and all Your hopes.
Guide me with your wisdom and Your laws.
Show me forgiveness for my failings.
Help me see my path in the midst of chaos.
Remember me when I am overcome in the darkness.
Walk at my side and remind me of Your strength.
Give me a forgiving heart and an understanding mind.
Make me aware of the suffering of others.
Lift me up to act against prejudice and ignorance.
Follow my days of trials ahead, to show me what path to take
        that leads to You.
My faith is in You always.
My hope depends on You always.
My heart is Yours always.

12.   Does the enemy tempt your heart?
Does he twist your good sense?
Is confusion common as you walk your path?
Is doubt plaguing your strength in your talent?
Guard your heart, only letting the Lord in.
Be confident in Godly wisdom.
Keep your mind sharp with worship and praise.
Use the talent gifted to you, never doubting God's choice.
Only with the Lord can you be who He wants you to be.
The enemy fails with the faithfulness and the goodness of our
    God.

13.   I've seen the evil man inflicts on man.
I've heard the questioning of God's goodness when tragedy comes.
I've seen the agony of people feeling punished due to disease.
I've seen the lost, grasping for the things of this world.
Don't allow the trappings of this world to allow you to doubt
    God's goodness.
Don't allow evil to become your focus. God will not allow it
    forever.
Don't believe tragedy and disease is what God wants for you.
Grow in the challenge when God allows suffering.
Pray for the lost, for God does not forsake the one that seeks
    Him.
Take heart in knowing all things of this world can be overcome
    and put to rest by our Lord.
He alone can make our path straight.
He alone can bring you peace beyond all understanding.

14.   I've climbed mountains and walked valleys,
You, Lord, were always there.
When my heart was heavy and I was lost in this world,
You, Lord, were always there.
You hear my song, You hear my praise.
You don't close Your ears to my sorrows.
How do I honor Your faithfulness?

You give so much and take nothing.
We are strong *only* with You.

15. Praise with voice in song.
Give praise with the keyboard and guitar.
Make music to honor our Lord Jesus.
Make sounds of joy and celebration.
Let your heart be peaceful in worship and praise.
All to our Saviour, the giver of salvation and peace.

16. War threatening like dark clouds before the storm.
Too often violence becoming the way over peace.
No regard for homes or lives. Governments lost, with only
power as the goal.
The God of faithfulness, mercy and love not consulted to
guide.
Only God can determine justice. Only God can deliver us.
But first we must ask.

17. Our Lord searched the shadows, not for the righteous but for
the lost.
He searched the shadows, not for the healthy but for the sick
and lame.
The shadows searched for the blind, opening eyes to see His
glory.
Out of the shadows of sin, He brought His light of redemption.
Don't hide in the shadows. Let yourself be found.
Then emerge into the light of salvation.

18. The sacrifice made, suffering beyond human understanding.
Sins taken on for all time for the people of this world then,
now, and forever more.
Grace present for the asking. The price already paid.
We aren't deserving of such forgiveness, love, and mercy.
The Lord's love, enough for Him to give such a gift.

He does not ask for it to be earned. Our love and devotion
    lacking. Yet grace and salvation free for the asking.
Our sins unforgivable, yet He forgives. Our lives broken,
    veering off course. Only the Lord can make our path
    straight.
We should focus on Him, yet we focus on this world.
The focus must be on our Lord Jesus, on His teaching of the
    new covenant. Focus on a journey with salvation freely
    given.
Simply believe in the One that made the sacrifice never again
    to be repeated. The salvation available to all mankind
    for all time, until our Lord returns.

19.   Do not hide malice in your heart.
Do not put efforts into being of this world.
This is not our home, we are simply passing through.
Be cautious not to become too deeply rooted in this world.
Keep shallow roots for easy transition.
We need to be alert to the calling of the Lord.
We cannot hear Him if we become too embedded in this life.
Our walk is completed in the blink of an eye.
Don't let it be laden with the treasures and ways of this world.
The longer you carry the weight, the more difficult to shed.
Therefore, don't allow your treasure to become your God.
The Lord Jesus is our treasure.

20.   The losses compounded by a viral plague.
Forewarned, a price will be paid for disregarding sin and stray-
    ing from the path we were set upon.
Consequences will come for injustice.
Truth being hidden by the glitz of this world.
We're blinded by its shine and promise.
We become heavy-laden by the weight of riches.
Love, a word used for promotion and perversion.
The Lord's love, our hope, our solace.
The Lord's faithfulness, our strength, our comfort.

The Lord's mercy, our salvation, our healing.
The Lord's goodness, our chance to survive.

21.   Sing songs of praise, sing songs of worship.
Say prayers of praise, say prayers of worship.
Fall on bended knee with honor and praise.
Fall on bended knee with repentance and thanksgiving.
Raise arms with cries of halleluiah.
Raise arms reaching out for mercy.
All brings glory to the ear of Jesus.
All brings us to the Father's arms.

22.   Let our words be true and just.
Let our service be founded on love not duty.
Let our counsel be with Godly wisdom.
Let our hospitality be warm and inviting.
Let our journey be led by the Lord.
Let our hearts be guarded by the Lord.
Let our touch be gentle and kind.
Let our lives reflect God's love.

23.   If you are weary, take rest in the word of Jesus.
If you are lost, seek guidance in the word of Jesus.
If you are joyous, praise God with the word of Jesus.
If you are conflicted, seek clarity from the word of Jesus.
If you are grateful, praise God with the word of Jesus
If you are sorrowful, seek comfort through the word of Jesus.
If you are angry, seek calm through the word of Jesus.
If you are burdened, seek relief through the word of Jesus.
If you are frustrated, seek enlightenment through the word of
    Jesus.
If you are confused, seek knowledge through the word of Jesus.
If you feel unwanted or unloved, embrace and accept the love
    of Jesus.

24. Doubts plague when we forget Your strength.
We stumble when we lose Your balance, Lord.
Heartache lingers when we can't see Your light.
When this world becomes too important to us, we can find strength in the power of Jesus.
We can only find level ground with the balance of Jesus.
His light heals hearts and gives peace.
Jesus can focus your eyes on Him and not the world.
We can't travel this life without knowing who is our strength, balance, and light.
Our peace will always be found in the love and guidance of Jesus.

25. Don't deny Jesus because mankind has remained misguided as were the Pharisees. They changed God's laws to suit their wants. Many today have become the false teachers Jesus warned us about. They pick and choose the parts of His word that justifies their agenda. It is often used to justify hate and judgement. They do not look at the entirety of His word.

They do not accept God's character that is evident in His word. His unchanging character has driven Him to be patient with the ones He created with so much love. The same love that drove the Father to send the Son. The Son that walked as a man and died for our sins. His mercy remains evident as He heals today, just as He did when He walked on earth. His faithfulness remains evident seen in continued blessings and answered prayers. We may not get what we want but we must trust in God's infinite wisdom.

That wisdom is applied to all his decisions. We can not put a limit on God's knowledge or wisdom. God's character of goodness, forgiveness and faithfulness should be accepted as our own and shown to God and man. His character of mercy, compassion and honesty must be accepted and made a way of living our lives. We must embrace truth, justice and honor as our banner. We must incorporate God's greatest characteristic of love in our life.

Love God, love others, love yourself. Be gracious to others. Emulate the grace God extends to us. Grace is being patient when it is difficult. Do not follow false teachers. Do not dismiss the one relationship that has eternal ramifications. Do not limit God to the finite knowledge we have of Him.

God is too vast, too great and too wise for us to comprehend. Accept the Son, the salvation and the grace so freely given. Trust in the guidance of the Holy Spirit. Trust in God's character. Trust that you are loved.

26. Prophecy told of His coming. Prophecy fulfilled with His arrival.
Rejected because expectations not met.
Expecting a soldier, not a baby in a manger.
Expecting Rome to be conquered, not sin to be conquered.
His love so massive, not recognized. It took miracles for eyes to be opened.
It took His sacrifice to save the sinner.
It took rising from the grave to convince us of His extraordinary love.
It took His followers to take His word to the world.
It took a broken world to find a need for Him.
In Him, redemption found, hope restored.
Hope remains in the word Jesus left with us.
The Holy Spirit sent to be our guide.
No blessings, no peace, no love, ever seen at the level Jesus brought that led to redemption.

27. "I give you peace." "Go in peace."
He gives us the peace that is beyond all understanding.
Peace is the calm that comes with serenity.
Serenity comes when you allow peace in your heart.
It is a product of the Lord's love, goodness, and mercy that gives us peace.
Peace is not just the absence of war.
Peace is actively giving a gift that frees the heart and soul.

It opens our eyes to the one that brought us peace.
The Prince of peace, the savior for all mankind, Jesus.
For in His salvation comes true eternal peace.
Now go and let peace be with you.
Then await the final, complete peace Jesus will establish after
    correcting all wrong, removing evil, and establishing
    His kingdom when He returns.

28.   The sun rises and the sun sets with lives lived in between.
Some accepting the guidance of the Lord.
Some walking their path alone with no comfort, no clarity,
    just chance at their side.
The straight path wanted for you. For the asking, the Lord
    Jesus will walk by your side.
He will let the Holy Spirit be your guide. He will give you peace.

29.   Peace can only come through faithfulness.
Knowing our Lord leads to knowing love.
Reading His word brings enlightenment.
Sharing His word furthers His kingdom.
Furthering His kingdom elevates mankind.
Mankind, God's creation, had lost its way.
The path restored after much sacrifice.
It is a path offered to all, price already paid.

30.   Pray in quiet with thoughts gathered.
Pray in the open with praise given.
Pray while hidden in your own sanctuary.
On your knees in the position of honor, pray.
When seated and your heart calls, pray.
For redemption, with gratitude and joy, pray.
Pray in sorrow, with comfort given.
No matter the prayer, all is heard.
Answered with His infinite perspective.
All heard by God, the One True God, whose Son answered
    our greatest prayer.

He brings forgiveness, and the promise of His presence in our
lives eternally.

31. This world, so busy, so bombarded by social media.
Can you hear yourself think? Can you find rest in the chaos?
True rest must be centered on the only one who will give us
eternal rest.
Focus your rest on praise. Focus your rest on worship.
Rest can only come in the arms of Jesus. Any other rest is
fleeting.
Our connection to Him is not the phone, computer, or
television.
Our connection is prayer and reverent conversation with the
Father and the one sent, the Son.
With the Holy Spirit our guide, true rest will come for the
weary and for the broken.
He can silence the mind from wrong influence.
Light and calm, He will bring to the soul.
Rest will come in the transference of God's love to each and
every one who will ask.

32. When you awake with the rising sun, give praise to the One
who allowed it.
When you go about your day, give praise to the One who
guides you.
When the trials come and sorrow enters, give praise to the
One who sustains us.
For mistakes made and lessons learned, give praise to the One
who forgives us.
As the day turns to night and quiet comes, give praise for the
peace we're given.
For every minute you take a breath, give praise to the One
who created us.
Let no time pass, no opportunity ignored, give praise to the
One who saved us.
Life continues, since sacrifice given, give praise to our dear Jesus.

33. Jesus came to give us a new start, a chance for Gentiles and
       Jews.
     To be put on a path leading to salvation, we would have new
       guidance, a new covenant.
     Peace is the reward that comes with redemption.
     The peace that leads your heart to follow the One True King.
     To allow His teachings to be a standard to live by, a standard
       guiding us and elevating mankind.
     God, as our first love, and our neighbor as our second.
     Changing our nature leading us to service from the heart.
     Never a forced servitude, but a *new* heart to love and care for
       our neighbors.
     A new heart that allows love as a motivator with priority to
       service.
     His example when coupled with His word will show us our
       failings.
     See His love for all, when once there were those considered to
       be enemies.
     See His compassion, watch Him heal, see His love for the
       beggar.
     He came from the Father, to rescue the lost, to teach God's love.
     He shows us His mercy, His goodness, His grace.
     Jesus came to give us a new start, a gift for Gentile and Jew.
     Salvation had come to the sinner and the righteous.
     The One True King, our Savior, the Lord Jesus, came to us.
     He came to save mankind.

34. Hope, the reward given for sacrifice.
     Joy, the reward given because of resurrection.
     Peace, the reward given with salvation.
     Love, the reward given from Your word.
     You, Lord Jesus, are the reward given.

35. The heart pumps life-sustaining oxygen.
     It keeps our bodies functioning.
     What of our mind and soul?

The oxygen feeds the brain, allowing the mind to function.
How are you sustaining your soul?
Oxygen, not a factor in touching the soul.
To breathe life into the soul, it must come from the redeemer,
   Lord Jesus.
The love, faithfulness, and mercy of Jesus is the oxygen of the
   soul.
Only can the soul remain whole with His word being its
   nutrition.
The word will be sustenance for the soul, as food is to the
   body.
It brings light to the spirit, comfort for your sorrows, and rest
   for your body and soul.
With His word, Jesus will sustain you.

36.   God, You freed Your people, led by Moses, Aaron, and Joshua.
      Mistakes made, sins committed. It took a second generation to
         be allowed into Your promised land.
      It took eating of its bounty before the manna ceased.
      Always faithful God, You never abandoned Your people.
      Struggling with keeping Your covenant, they made many mistakes.
      You knew century after century people would fail.
      Your love and faithfulness stronger than Your laws.
      Because of the greatness of Your love, You sent us Your heart.
      You sent us Your Son, as a lamb to the slaughter.
      You sent with Him a *new* covenant.
      He sacrificed all to carry our sins away, yet many still did not
         believe.
      We still fail in our walk, yet Your grace now given.
      We await Your final return Jesus, the promise we can antici-
         pate with hope.

37.   We praise You, Lord, in the suffering.
      You draw us close as we grow with Your love.
      With Your mercy, we know physical pain is a temporary state,
         only of this world.

Spiritual pain can be eternal if we don't follow You.
You use what we bring upon ourselves in this world, to allow
us to become more dependent on You, Lord.
Eternal peace and grace *can* be our final reward.
We cannot have the door opened if we do not knock.
We cannot be found if we continue to deny the shepherd's
voice.
The greatest gift is Your love and sacrifice made.
Accepting that gift is like drinking from heaven's spring.
The water of life, forever flowing in our soul.
We are grateful for Your faithfulness in pursuing us.
Grateful for your love that saves us.
Grateful, knowing all suffering will end in Your loving arms.

38.   Amidst man's misguided ways, our Lord, You draw us near.
Finding things of this world to be our gods, our Lord, You
remain near.
Never leaving us without the Holy Spirit, our Lord, You
remain faithful.
Wanting us to accept the price paid, our Lord, Your love ever
present.
With souls hanging in the balance, our Lord, Your mercy
remains.
Seeing man's inhumanity to man, our Lord, You remain
patient.
Will we ever come to our senses? Our Lord, always our hope.
How can we deny Your sacrificial love?
Lord, open our eyes to You and help us learn Your word.
Guide us to accept the salvation won, the price paid.
Hope, peace, and knowledge given, Lord, draw us near.
Remind us of the choice that will lead us to You.
Lord Jesus, draw us near.

39.   The infant, innocent, helpless, needs total care.
The infant will grow, becoming less dependent as a child.
The child will grow to an independent adult.

We must return to complete dependence.
Not for physical needs but for spiritual needs.
The needs too often overlooked.
The needs we merely think sustained by *being spiritual.*
Society brands spirituality as being good and believing in a
      higher power.
Who is their *higher power*, not given a name?
What conclusions does *being spiritual* bring?
Does it conclude on earth?
Where is their savior in this Babylon world we live in?
To what end is doing good, without the heart of Jesus?
Become dependent on the character of God.
The characteristics, realized in the Son.
The Son, our salvation from the captivity of this world.
The Son, liberating us from obsession of self.
The Son, our treasure, more valuable than gold or jewels.
Instill His word in your heart.
With the word, spirituality comes from the Holy Spirit.
Your reward no longer uncertain, salvation will come with
      belief in the Son.
Spirituality from Jesus leads to eternal life.

40.   The Father gave His promise with the rainbow.
The Son gave His promise with His blood.
The Holy Spirit gives His promise when Christ received.
The Holy Trinity gives the promise of a world that can be
      saved.

41.   The Samaritan woman you saw as one of Your own.
The blind man You saw, then showed him Your light.
The woman who sinned, You saw as a reason for Your coming.
The son brought back to life, You saw as a gift to his mother.
The tax collector, You saw as a part of Your mission.
The woman of faith You saw, allowing her to be healed by her
      faith, at the touch of Your robe.
You saw the world, You saw the needs.

You see us with that same mercy even now.

42.   My life was guided by the calling You gave.
A life blessed by following your call as a nurse.
A man's love sent to restore my life.
That love taken back to you and growing my faith.
An illness allowed, isolating me in Your word.
Baptized, renewing my devotion to You.
The gift of Your calling, retained at a level to provide my
      earthly father's care.
Remaining in Your care, illness present still.
Your love allowed my heart to be given on a mission.
A mission changing my heart forever, the people never to leave
      my soul.
Then healed, Your love seen, so faithful and pure.
Let me bring glory to the Holy Trinity.
Your love, so ever-present, so ever-merciful.
Your character can not be challenged.
You, Lord, pour it out on a broken world and on the broken
      person.
You restore hope, restore lives, renewing faith in the faithful.
Bringing salvation as an offering to all.
I praise You, my dear sweet Jesus.
I will always worship You, my redeemer.

43.   You walk at our side, yet Your footprints are not seen.
Your comfort present, even when we forget Your promise.
You make our path straight even when we forget to ask.
You continue sending blessings, hoping we acknowledge them.
You lift us up out of our sin, even when we aren't certain You hear.
Forgiveness given for the asking, grace the gift for the sacrifice
      You made.
Such love, not known before. Such love, always present.
I praise Your name above all others.
Jesus my love, my hope, my life.

44.　A world plagued with materialism and self-gratification.
A world of leaders seeking domination.
A world of intolerance and injustice.
We know You do not want this for us.
Many know You and follow You but are quiet in their
　　knowledge.
Our duty, to teach others Your word, so to You they can turn.
We praise Your goodness, we praise Your wisdom.
Grateful to be safe in Your love and salvation.

45.　I will praise You in the morning and in the noonday sun.
I will praise You in the evening until the night is done.
I will praise You in song and in words spoken in prayer.
I will raise my praise to You, Lord, forever and ever.

46.　As children learning to walk and speaking our first words,
You teach us how to love, and with that You are heard.
The lessons written down, from the time You walked on earth,
Teaching forgiveness, love, and how we all have worth.
Your miracles and sacrifice, the world changed by Your touch.
You came for the sinner, to allow him righteousness.
By Your hand we are healed, with Your blood You took our sin.
Now when we learn and live the word, our life can then begin.

47.　With nations ravaged by war, and famine plaguing others.
We see the price we pay, for denying we all are brothers.
Lessons taught and lives lost, all tells us how to live.
Will we never listen, Lord? What price will we give?
Evil still remains, spiritual warfare one path it takes.
Lord, I know it won't be forever, since You paid for our
　　mistakes.
You said You would return someday, then evil's time is done.
We must listen and heed Your word, or death will surely come.
If eternal life is what we want, just one path we can take.
Accept the Lord Jesus, then a path for you He'll make.

48.   Our joy we have from You, Lord, a deep sense of life assured.
       Our lives can now be free, Lord, our nature can be cured.
       We no longer walk alone, Lord, from our sins we can be free.
       With resurrection came such joy, for the price You paid for
              me.

49.   You promised us salvation, yet You gave us so much more.
       Your character sustains us, given us at our core.
       In the great creation, Your image did come through.
       It lies in Your character, in us strong and true.
       To draw upon Your mercy, so freely You did give,
       It should open our eyes to suffering, helping others live.
       Your love so overwhelming, we have seen it in the Son.
       With that love and mercy, we saw salvation won.
       Your love in us instilled, we must draw from such power.
       We must show each other love with every given hour.
       With faithfulness maintained, from the Father to the Son.
       We must remain faithful, for in Jesus victory is won.
       So patient, kind, and truthful, when in this world You showed
              so much.
       Can such patience, truth, and kindness, ever be found in us?
       With Your goodness, justice, and forgiveness, from these You
              never waver.
       Our character buried deep, will it ever gain Your favor?
       We thank You for such character that remains in us deep inside.
       Bring forth Your character in us Lord, so in you we can abide.

50.   Lord, I see You in creation, the sun and moon and stars.
       It proves to me You're near, never very far.
       The stately rose, the pansy's face, so precious are to me.
       You give us fragrant flowers, many colors for us to see.
       Each animal, bird and fish, You so tenderly measured.
       Each one precious in Your eyes, every one Your treasure.
       You tolerate our path, no matter how we stray off course.
       With each correction made, we feel Your divine force.
       Of all Your creation, it is man that brought You pain.

We failed time after time, Your patience may be in vain.
So You sacrificed all, to make certain we have a chance.
Believing in the price paid, our lives You then enhance.
So we praise Your name and for forgiveness we ask.
In all of creation Lord, man is Your greatest task.

51.   You said, Lord, "I am the way."
You are the way to our redemption.
You are the way to the Father.
You said, Lord, "I am the truth."
Your truth is a new covenant; it is Your word.
Not brought by force, but brought by love.
That love is the truth given to all mankind.
You said, Lord, "I am the life."
Life comes to us through Your truth.
Your truth shows us the way to eternal life.
Yes, Lord, You are the way, the truth, the life.
I rejoice in Your word, our truth.
It remains our guide to the way.
It is the gift of eternal life.

52.   Praise, praise, we give You praise.
Down on our knees with hands raised.
Love, love, we give You our love, for the family here and up above.
Song, song, we sing Your song, it gives us strength to know we
        belong.
Worship we give, in worship we come, knowing salvation is
        surely won.
Joy, joy, You bring us joy, sending angels to each girl and boy.
You are ever present, with grace You give.
My heart is Yours, Lord, with Your grace I live.

53.   Blessings, ever-present, freely flowing, even in difficult
times of loss and pain. Your blessings, Lord, do not stop flowing. Your comfort, insight, strength, and love remain. Open
our eyes to the blessings of air to breathe, warmth of the sun,

each new day. Open our eyes to acknowledge the miracle of birth, the wonder of a child's curiosity. These are blessings all.

Make us see the blessing of being able to eat, walk, and talk. Make us see the blessings of people helping people and neighbor helping neighbor. Help us acknowledge Your blessing of the freedom to worship Your name openly and at will. You, Lord Jesus, never stop handing out the blessings of a friendly smile or a kind word.

You, Lord, remind us of the glory of Your goodness, love, forgiveness, and grace. Each are monumental blessings. You heal, You strengthen, You answer prayer. You walk at our side, direct our path, and open our eyes to injustice. Everyone a blessing given merely because of Your faithfulness and mercy. We are lost if we do not come to You with thanksgiving and praise for the blessing of such love.

54. When you are frightened and alone,
Call on the name of Jesus.
When you are ill and feeling pain,
Call on the name of Jesus.
When injustice and evil is in your path,
Call on the name of Jesus.
When you are lost and hope is gone,
Call on the name of Jesus.
When your grief is overwhelming and will not cease,
Call on the name of Jesus.
For a life full of peace and salvation won,
Call on the name of Jesus.

55. I greet each day with thanksgiving and praise.
To You, our Lord, my heart is raised.
Elevated to a glorious height, Your spirit soars.
You sent the Holy Spirit, to remain in our core.
How did we ever exist before You came?
It wasn't enough to just praise Your name.
It took all that You had to give us a new life.

It took all You gave to relieve our strife.
Tears come in gratitude and in praise.
Tears still come for the price Jesus paid.
I pray to You, for in You is my strength.
Strength is given at such a great length.
Never in life could I do this alone.
Thank You, Holy Spirit, You guide us home.

56.   Laughter, joy, and happiness abound
It's in You, Jesus, such love is found.
We see it in newborn lambs in spring.
The joy of life, only You bring.
We see it in a summer rain,
We hear it in each hymn's refrain.
We can walk this land in peace and light.
Jesus in You comes such Holy might.

57.   You see beauty in the young and old.
You see beauty in scars still bold.
You see beauty in the lame and lost.
You see beauty, no matter the cost.
Never do You think one of us not Yours.
Never do You think their spirit can't soar.
Never do You give up on each life.
We praise You, Lord, for Your sacrifice.

58.   Why do you remove from this life such strife?
Why do you give us a chance at new life?
We disappoint and fail each day that goes by, no matter inten-
        tions or how hard we try.
By Your grace You save, by Your grace You heal, salvation You
        brought and Your love is real.
To let others know of this glorious gift given, we must tell of
        Your death, then how You were risen.
It isn't right to not share the story of such grace.
We must be certain all know, to take their place.

For by Your side we all can walk, because of You our salvation
    bought.

59.   You healed me Lord when I did not ask.
You healed my son, when I begged for the task.
I know how freely Your love is given.
I know when asked, sins are forgiven.
We don't always know why Your choices are made.
We can trust in You, Your character won't fade.
To praise You, Lord, seems so little to give.
Guide my words, to teach others to live.
It is from Your word, we will find Your direction.
From Your word, we know Your expectations.
How will we know if we are never told?
It's in Your truth, our hearts should be bold.
Take a chance and tell the story of our Lord.
Salvation only given, if the story is told.

60.   When solitude weighs heavy in the quiet of the night, Lord, you are present to comfort and reassure. As the chaos of this world becomes too loud, you bring quiet reassurance to my soul. Seeing acts of hate and violence becoming quietly accepted, Lord, You hear the cries for justice. Just when I become over burdened with the grief of innocent lives lost, You, my Lord, reassure me of Your faithfulness. Jesus, You experienced the solitude, the chaos, the violence and loss. You overcame it all in the body of a man. You brought redemption, grace and unfailing love. Help me remember that You are my ever present peace, comfort and salvation.

61.   What can we say about such sacrifice and loss?
What can we say about the extraordinary cost?
What can we say about such suffering and pain?
What can we say about what we can gain?
There is only one word to the Lord needs spoken.
It will heal your soul and all who are broken.
The word so simple it's not a great task.

Say *yes* to Christ Jesus and forgiveness ask.

62.   Evil reaps no reward, its path dark, void of light.
It knows not peace or the goodness of love given.
Do not take such a path following the dark.
Turn to the Lord, to the direction of love, life, peace, and
    redemption.
Don't allow darkness to remove the light.
The choice is yours alone.
Only the Lord can protect us from the dark.
Only He has the power to defeat all evil.

63.   I rest in Your love, Lord, my heart filled with peace.
Only in You, Lord, will contentment not cease.
So little in this life is so very dear.
You bring hearts together, teaching love without fear.
With Your guidance we are blessed, it's love You choose.
It's the kind of love, we can never lose.
It reminds us, there is no love greater than Yours.
It is a gift given, making hearts soar.
You, my Lord, taught us how to love.
You are dear Lord, our gift from above.

64.   Jesus, You rode into the city on a lowly colt, not a mighty
    steed.
You rode over a street covered with palms, not a street paved
    with gold.
The King of Kings wore the clothing of a peasant not the royal
    robes of a true king.
Crowned with thorns, not jewels.
Jeered and taunted, not praised and worshiped.
Lord, you allowed all of this.
You chose the weakness of the human form.
Yet here we are complaining about discomforts often brought
    upon ourselves.
We continue to sin, accepting lies as a normal standard.

We continue to witness man's inhumanity to man.
We are undeserving of all You did and all You are.
Yet Lord, You continue to be patient and forgiving.
You are the one perfect example of love, mercy and compassion.
You forgive the unforgivable, love those considered unloveable, and have mercy on the hopeless.
Instill the strength needed to continue the journey and commitment to glorify Your name.
Give me the wisdom to share Your word, and forgiveness when I fail.
Let others see Your light in my spirit.
Your grace sustains me, Your love elevates me, and Your faithfulness nurtures me.
So undeserving of the humble King who saw us worth saving.
I praise Your goodness and Your name, King Jesus.

65.   We know the stories of God's wrath and correction.
We know His works to correct our direction.
When it didn't work a new path He took, to sacrifice His son, foretold in His book.
Prophets of old, told of His plan to come.
They put into writing, the preparation done.
Then as we learn, how the story unfolds.
It becomes even greater than what was told.
Never had we thought, the extent of His love, would bring such healing and redemption to us.
God's plan enormous in its scope, realizing in sin, we could no longer cope.
We thank You, Father, for the Son.
Told in the beginning salvation would come.

66.   What miracle would you want to see?
So many were witnessed yet quickly forgotten.
Too numerous to count but so easily dismissed.
Jesus showed He was God, yet denied.
Man's finite mind just seeing the man.

Even though His resurrection was witnessed by so many,
        instead of rejoicing lies spread to hide its fact.
He died to take away our sin, still resistance seen.
The miracle I want to see is that the eyes of man would be
        opened.

67.   For each morning I rise, for each night I rest,
       Lord, You are my strength each day and peace each night.
       For everyday of joy, for every trial of sorrow,
       Jesus, You are my contentment and resolve.
       I walk with assurance, run in freedom, all because of You.
       Blessed, challenged, growing in faith with Your hand upon
               me.
       With Your voice in my ears, Your touch on my heart, and Your
               conviction in my soul, I live.
       Grace You extend to me.
       Mercy You have given me.
       Love You pour out on me.
       I give all to You in word, thought, and deed.
       Guide me in all ways to bring glory and honor to You.

68.   We did not ask, yet You knew our need.
       The Father knew, with His son, we would be freed.
       Your love for us, so pure and clean.
       You wanted our sinful souls redeemed.
       To provide the cleansing that was needed, You came to us, the
               Father's wish heeded.
       You knew the price to give us good news.
       Knowing the cost, still You did choose.
       Undeserving, with all lost in our sin, God knew with You, new
               life could begin.
       Precious Jesus, prophecy You fulfilled.
       Precious Jesus, hated and killed.
       The Father's plan was not yet done.
       For after death, He raised His Son.
       Such love and mercy, never before seen.

With sacrifice made, all can be redeemed.
Just remember though, when all is done, you must believe in
    the Lord, then salvation is won.
Then keep hope in your heart and never despair, for when
    Jesus returns, we'll remain in His care.

69.   Perfect love, known at creation, God gives throughout time.
Merciful, God saved His people time after time.
Then the Father sent the Son, salvation truly won.
Perfect love, oh so pure, a love man didn't deserve.
Through much sacrifice this love was given.
Love for Gentile and Jew, when Christ was risen.
A love no longer Israel's alone.
Now we all are His, as of one home.
God's children are now, all who believe.
The Son of God set all nations free.

70.   Do not disregard the wisdom of Our Creator.
You, Lord, brought us wisdom in Your word.
That wisdom tells us to fear God.
Not merely to make us cower, but to recognize God's power.
Not just to fear enough to bow in submission,
But to bow in worship and praise.
Respect the power of the One who spoke the world into
    existence.
Fear and respect the One that heals with word or touch.
The same One who has the power to rid all evil, or eliminate
    all creation.
Power, man claims to have, yet it's wielded as a weapon for
    personal gain.
God's power used to bring us redemption with the resurrection.
Do not challenge or test God.
Fear the One who sent the Son. Be obedient to Our Creator.
Let that obedience be out of love not fear. Let fear lead you to
    request Godly wisdom.
That wisdom leads to redemption.

That redemption leads to life.
That life becomes eternal.

71. For Your faithfulness, Father, I give You praise.
For Your mercy, Jesus, my worship I raise.
For Your guidance, Holy Spirit, I praise Your way.
With Your word, Lord, lives can be saved.
With Your word, Lord, we learn mercy and goodness.
With Your word, Lord, we learn You don't forsake us.
With Your word, Lord, new life is given.
Because of You, Lord, voices of praise rise to heaven.

72. Praise, praise, we sing Your praise.
We write it down in hymns refrain.
Our hearts continue to sing with joy.
We write children's praise for girls and boys.
The praise of Jesus should be on our tongue.
Praise to His glory continuously sung.
Each song we write should praise His name.
With song and praise our hearts will change.
Don't let a single day simply pass you by.
To the Son of God, let praise be our cry.
Never in this life can enough praise arise.
Once sacrifice was done, the Lord did rise.
So praise His name and the love He gives.
Jesus, our Lord, came for us to live.

73. The cross, rugged and harsh it stood.
The man, too tender, gracious, and good.
His blood kept falling to the ground.
At His feet, His grieving mother was found.
No such pain could a mere man endure.
His body was man, but His heart was pure.
No sin did this precious soul commit.
At the right hand of God, our Lord would sit.
But first unimaginable suffering came to Him.

Never such suffering would we see again.
It had to be done, it's the price He would pay.
In order to save man, He took our sins away.
Don't let this sacrifice be done in vain.
Believe in His love, for such a price paid.
Know in your heart, when He arose from the grave,
    it was each of you, our Lord came to save.

74.   A blinding light You shown on a sinner.
He became Your disciple from Your transformation.
Sacrifices made to tell Your truth.
Truth often rejected to remain of this world.
Shine Your transformative light again, on those in darkness.
Keep the path lit for those who want to seek Your light.
Remain as a light in me to share with the world.

75.   The baby wrapped in swaddling clothes,
    becomes the man, dying exposed.
The man healing and giving so much,
    brought light to all He touched.
There truly are not enough words to state,
    the joy of redemption, His sacrifice made.
We now have His word, for a guide today.
Each word He spoke to lead the way.
A way with a new covenant was given.
The Son was God's plan for a way to heaven.
The Son did not fail, He met all our needs.
We're no longer tied to endless creeds.
None of this matters, if we reject His gift.
Without belief in the Son, eternal life we will miss.

76.   In the darkness, You are the light.
In the light, You are our hope.
When we fall, You lift and hold us tight.
When we cry out, You hear and know.
From our lowest depth, compassion You show.

From our highest peaks, You rejoice.
We don't walk alone unless by our choice.
You never forsake us, unless our denial is clear.
You always wait for us to draw near.
Forgiveness freely given, when our repentance You hear.

77.   We all are broken in this world that we walk.
We are swaying in the wind, like a broken cornstalk.
No direction or path are we given when we begin.
It is a learning curve, some will lose, yet some will win.
Man alone let temptation take Paradise from us all.
Man allowed sin to enter, allowing us to fall.
After God did His best to correct our path to Him,
He then called upon the Son, letting new life begin.
No matter that salvation is won from the sacrifice He gave.
The only thing that matters is belief in Him to be saved.

78.   Why do so many deny You? In their sin, do they want to stay?
Why do so many defy You? Can't they simply walk Your way?
Why do so many distrust You? Is your story too good to be
      true?
Why are You overshadowed? Are earthy treasures brighter than
      You?
Why can't they hear truth spoken? Are they deaf to all but lies?
How long will they stumble and risk their eternal lives?
The answers I don't know Lord, but from You I will not stray.
You forgive my many sins, in Your salvation I will stay.

79.   When you sing a song of praise, be certain to whom praise is
      given.
Do not praise the things of a broken world, but raise your
      praise to heaven.
This world is not the eternity promised, we must find our way
      to You.
Leaving old ways behind, Your ways are honest and true.

It is not simple to walk Your path, yet You guide us in Your
    way.
We must focus our time on Your word, and close to You we
    can stay.
We must believe in the savior that came to set us all free.
Jesus, we must trust in You, or Your glory will never be seen.

80.   His disciples were shown their path by the Lord, some more
    faithful than others.
They had three years before He would leave, then He would
    send another.
The Holy Spirit would come to all that believed.
In the name of Jesus the word was received.
Taught to Jew and Gentile alike, the word the apostles spread.
To all nations and all people alike, in each language the word
    was said.
He continues to this day to be the giver of new life.
His word in this world telling His story of sacrifice.

81.   He carried His cross, body broken, pain intense.
Simon then lifted the cross and gave His body rest.
This sinless man led, like a lamb to the slaughter.
His mother at His side, the painful burden upon her.
Some disciples ran away, yet one stayed at His side.
"Take my mother, John," He said. John would then abide.
Blood flowing, body shredded, the sight unbearable to see.
We cannot fathom the physical pain He suffered for you and
    me.
Only that was not enough for His job to be complete.
Taking on the sins of all mankind, our sins He would defeat.
All the suffering, all the cost, to one pure and selfless man.
Means nothing without belief, with faith salvation is at hand.
Jesus walked this earth, fully God and fully man.
Bringing salvation to mankind was the Father's plan.
Read His story and study His word, please take it all to heart.
Just believe in Jesus the Christ, then from Him never part.

82.   His mercy so great, to return a child from death.
His forgiveness overwhelming, as each one confessed.
His love deep and abiding, as He healed the sick and lame.
His character never changing, for this is why He came.
His justice was like none had seen before.
He threw the money takers off the temple's floor.
The Samaritan woman, not a stranger to Him.
She was not the enemy, He forgave her sin.
It did not matter, beggar, tax collector or leper, each a person
     of His heart, each life made better.
From the time He spent walking on this earth, His goal always
     to bring people worth.
That commitment never changed, on earth or with the Father.
It still holds true today, in His love, His mercy, His honor.

83.   They walked by His side, to Emmaus they went.
They were telling this man of such a tragic event.
They were bothered by what happened, and they told Him so.
Not knowing who He was, along the road they did go.
They invited Him to dinner, to share their bread and wine.
When He broke the bread, He vanished before their eyes.
It was at that moment they knew who He was.
The risen Lord had walked with them, on the road to Emmaus.

84.   Their bodies ravaged by disease, some were also lame.
Many found they were healed, in our Lord's holy name.
Demons were removed, the way Jesus had taught.
The evil that possessed them, the apostles now fought.
Sins of every kind, now forgiven as grace was found.
Once a believer, the gift of grace abounds.
The apostles spread the word and healed along the way.
It was not an easy path, persecution the price paid.
The devotion remained strong, in the men Jesus trained.
No matter the sacrifice, in their Lord they remained.
They were true to the teachings and spread the good news.
It mattered not the cost, for Christ they did choose.

They saw what the Lord had sacrificed for them.
Committed to God's word, remaining true to Him.
The path was not easy, no easy path to bare.
Yet each and every one would remain in God's care.
So when your path becomes harder than you knew.
Remember God's apostles and what they did for you.

85.   Joy comes to those who know the Lord, peace comes to those
who believe.
Comfort comes from His written word, Godly wisdom ours
to receive.
With guidance and faith, we walk the path, the Holy Spirit
becomes our guide.
Salvation is ours if only we ask, it's God's love that we find.

86.   I write these Psalms to You, my Lord, such love You brought
to me.
Too many ways to count, my Lord, so much glory have I seen.
So many times I watched You heal, so often You took them home.
You blessed me with reassurance, none were left alone.
You honor prayer when not deserved, Your goodness with no
bounds.
It's in Your daily faithfulness, my confidence is found.
Your words will always touch my heart, no matter the age I
become.
Each time I reread Your stories, I know from Your love they
come.
So patient You are each time I fail, it's with Your guidance,
Lord, I avail.
You healed me when I did not ask, You allow me to write, a
beloved task.
Unknown, Lord, why so much love poured out on me.
Keep the light You gave me, shining bright to see.
I write these Psalms to You, my Lord, to honor all You are.
I want Your story told, my Lord, taken near and far.
No other love, so true and just, will they ever know.

For salvation and for peace in life, to You they must go.

87.   He bids you come to know His love, praise His holy name.
It takes your love to belong, praise His holy name.
Peace will come when salvation won, praise His holy name.
Grace He brings to all mankind, praise His holy name.

88.   Dusty sandals, weary legs, feet dirty from the road.
So many miles to spread the word, so many words to be told.
His robes would drag on the ground, collecting dirt and dust.
He did not look like a king, yet He humbly won their trust.
His followers began to grow, as the word He did spread.
No longer just to Jews He preached, but to everyone instead.
He wanted Jew and Gentile alike to know the gift He brought.
No longer could life remain as it was, the new covenant He
    then taught.
The first, to put God above all else, for us to find our way.
The second, to love your neighbor, these commands the stron-
    gest to say.
Too often we forget the impact on mankind Jesus made.
He took our sins for us to redeem, and His covenant would
    remain.

89.   Our Lord used the most unlikely to spread His word to man.
Jesus changed a persecutor of Jews, from Saul to Paul He
    became.
Blinded on the road to Damascus, this man was made to see.
Not just his sight restored, his heart changed, in Christ to be.
The Lord guided this man throughout his years to establish
    the church for Christ.
He suffered much yet never failed, his faith came at a price.
Our Lord can use anyone, His choice may not always be ours.
But with His choice, the way is paved to lead us to His arms.

90.   Once the Lord came to earth, patterns He began to change.
No longer hate your enemy, but in your prayer they should
      remain.
No longer should we worry, it will never bring reward your way.
No longer eye for an eye, in insult we must simply turn away.
Do not make a show of your prayer, just go to your room to pray.
He brought a kinder, gentler world if all would follow His way.
We must embrace His peace to live a better life for all.
So in this life with the Lord, just be sure to answer His call.

91.   The choice we make in this life will decide eternity.
Our choices in this life, only two choices can there be.
It sounds so simple to just say yes, but know what it means.
You are saying yes to the Son of God, and in Him you must
      believe.
With His sacrifice and resurrection, you must know the price
      He paid.
Accept the love and mercy that led Him to His grave.
Then know God's goodness when He came back to life.
Trust the word and grace that came at such a price.
Then choose our Lord and Savior, for His word is what you
      need.
Then for all eternity your soul will then be freed.

92.   Women and children, both great loves of the Lord.
Jesus honored them both, bringing them reward.
Never were they hidden in shadows, or merely passed by.
The children He drew near, the women, He heard their cry.
A lesson can be learned, from the compassion that He brought.
He knows everyone has value, this was the lesson He taught.
At the time Christ walked this earth, they were *the least of these.*
The Son of God elevated them, knowing they should be seen.

93.   Christ Jesus when He rose, first appeared to a woman.
This woman had been faithful, He honored her when risen.

The angels reminded her of the words Jesus said, telling on the
     third day He would rise from the dead.
Words came back to her, then no longer was it a surprise.
So hard to comprehend how a dead man could rise.
She then prepared the disciples, for He would soon go to them.
Faithful in His promise, it was clear it was truly Him.
Jesus honored this woman, Mary Magdalene was her name.
All mankind is included. For man, woman and child Jesus
     came.

94.   The sun warms my face, my hands, my heart.
       Lord, Your light is even brighter, never in us to part.
       The sun goes down, turning day to night.
       In You, Lord, never fading is eternal light.
       Your light so bright, it shines from within.
       The Holy Spirit our guide, Godly light in Him.
       Please open our hearts to the light you have given.
       It comes from Lord Jesus, when sins are forgiven.

95.   John the Baptist led the way, baptizing as he went,
       Preparing all who would listen to the One the Father sent.
       He then one day would baptize the Son.
       John's mission fulfilled, His salvation surely won.
       Jesus tempted in the wilderness then His ministry could begin.
       The battle with the devil, the Son certainly did win.
       Nothing would be easy for the Lord, to win against our sin.
       Nothing could stop Jesus, our salvation depended on Him.

96.   When you are weary, and your heart is heavy remember the
          beatitudes Christ said.
       His blessings and rewards upon you, if mournful or meek,
          He'd save.
       His blessings to the righteous, who were persecuted in His
          name.
       He blessed the hungry, the peacemakers, and to the pure of
          heart He came.

The merciful would find mercy, the falsely accused would find
    the same.
In His name, you will find salvation, in Him never to part.
All these promises with His great love present from the start.
Blessings are such a simple thing, yet they are everything to us.
No greater is the blessing that is You, Lord Jesus.

97.   The notes rise up in praise, to honor Him their voices raise.
In His love they rejoice, to follow Him is their choice.
If you don't feel love or peace, in praising God, you find relief.
So raise your voice to God above, raise your voice in song of
    love.
Rejoice for the mercy He gives, rejoice in the life we can live.

98.   You wept Lord, for the love of a friend, Your people, and a city.
Your heart You poured out for the love of so many.
Long grueling days, many miles walked, the Word spread each
    day.
Fatigue, heartache, suffering, being human this was the way.
As God, You allowed the journey to save all mankind.
As God, You allowed human form, knowing pain You'd find.
As God, Your character never wavered, the struggle and sacri-
    fice made.
As God, You fulfilled each prophecy, proving the Messiah
    truly came.
As God, You rose to save Your creation, denying none the gift
    given.
As God, You ask for belief, so we can join You in heaven.

99.   How can we measure Your goodness and strength?
Only one man walked, without sin in this place.
Man still can't believe You had no sin.
So many reject Your word, their heart's won't win.
The sinless, precious Son of God, came for us all.
Being tempted as man, You rejected evil's call.
If we must follow a man, let it be only You.

Having been man and being God, it's You we must choose.

100. Whenever doubts cloud your mind, remember the story of
      Thomas.
His doubts were strong but were eased when seeing the Lord's
      promise.
Some need to see with their own eyes before they truly believe.
Remember belief is in your heart, and God's love can make
      you see.
So never doubt the love of the Lord, no greater love can there be.
If you have doubts, simply be sure, the consequences they can
      bring.
Your most costly doubt could simply be, to reject the One
      True King.

101. You walked this world as man and God, fully both at one time.
You gave such compassion and mercy, Your work was so divine.
You wept at the grave of Lazarus, his sister's pain you could
      feel.
As God You would raise him from the grave, as man the grief
      was real.
With Your love and mercy, You saved so many lives.
As God, it was the Father's plan, as man Your heart so kind.
So often we forget, the price You paid each day.
As man You felt the suffering, as God You showed the way.

102. Wake and be joyful in the morning light.
Wake and give God the glory for another day.
Praise His name with a grateful heart and peaceful spirit.
Give praise for salvation won and life eternal.
Be heard in your joyous praise, not in public but to the ears of
      a loving God and merciful Savior.
Let him know the gift is received with gladness and hope.
Another day to praise and worship the One who allowed it.
A day we should not take lightly but rejoice in its light.
Rejoice in the light of Christ Jesus.

Take His light into the world with thanksgiving and joy.
Bathe yourself in the morning light.
Immerse yourself in the light of Christ.
Both are blessings from His love and goodness.
Both are gifts from a Holy God.

103. King David foretold Your coming, God's promise acknowledged.
He wrote praise to celebrate Your faithfulness as God, our Creator.
David faced and defeated a giant, yet not on his own.
You prepared him for the challenge God, giving him strength and courage to protect his flock from lion and bear.
God the Father, Jesus the Son, the Holy Spirit, all present for all time.
You, Lord Jesus, still today with the Father and Spirit.
Still today, You prepare us for our challenges.
In that preparation You grow our courage turning fortitude to faith and faith to fortitude.
Still today, as in the time of David, You are ever present.
Today, unlike David's time, we have the gift of salvation.
We have the knowledge of Your sacrifice and resurrection.
We received the promise foretold.
Jesus, the One True King, who took His place for all time.
I am grateful for the promise kept.
Your faithfulness unchanging, Your preparation and guidance never-ending.
Our Lord, our King, our Savior, came as foretold, as promised for all people for all time.

104. The Lamb of God came to be our guide.
He became the shepherd, His peace we'd find.
Our shepherd, we must know His voice.
To deny what is heard would be a poor choice.
As the shepherd guides His sheep, we must come when He speaks.

His love so strong, He'd leave the ninety-nine for one.
So devoted to the lost, He seeks and begs you to come.
Know the Lord's word, listen to what He says.
It is in His love, we all find rest.
So listen to the shepherd and come when He calls.
Only salvation comes from the Lord, offered to us all.

105.   The God that created the universe, knows every star in the sky.
He knows every person born by name, He knows every child's
     cry.
He knows each feather on the sparrow and each hair on your
     head.
Why does He want to know us, with such love we are led.
He watched us fail for so long, but His love over flowed.
The Father sent the Son, never before such love was shown.
It now allows us true salvation, from the sacrifice that was
     made.
The sacrifice for all mankind, for this our Savior came.

106.   The life we were given was not meant to be traveled on calm
     seas with sunny skies.
It is a journey meant to be traveled with divine guidance.
You will be blown about when gales come. You will need shel-
     ter in the storm.
Your joy will be dependent on the peace in your heart.
We weren't promised the perfect journey.
We were promised we don't have to travel it alone.
Your success of reaching journey's end intact, comes only in
     Lord Jesus.

107.   You cannot find courage if you have never been challenged to
     use it.
Don't let the challenge be met without the presence of the One
     with the greatest courage, used to save all mankind.
In Lord Jesus, any challenge can be met with courage.

Let Him remain at your side. We were not meant to win every
challenge, every contest, every battle alone.
Only with the strength, goodness, and mercy of our Lord
should we expect to find victory.
Find courage. Just find it in the One that loves you most. Find
courage in Christ Jesus.

108. I can cry tears of sorrow, or find joy that cannot part.
No matter where life leads, my Savior has my heart.
He never leaves my side, whether I celebrate or mourn.
He keeps heaping on more blessings, and my heart is reborn.
So personal the Savior, I can tell Him anything.
He offers friendship, to every single human being.
It's a friendship for a lifetime, a life never alone.
The One who knows your secrets, and gives your heart a home.
If you want a friend, who will never leave your side,
If you want a savior, where all sins are left behind,
I suggest you meet my friend, for He will also be yours.
His name is Christ Jesus, your best friend and your Lord.

109. You taught the lesson of the mustard seed so small of little
concern.
You told us of its growth, and of the lesson we could learn.
Telling us our faith can grow, from such a tiny start.
Knowing growth in faith also grows our heart.
The kingdom of heaven, founded on such faith, is massive in
expanse.
We are so blessed with Your wisdom, and how You give us a
chance.
The tiny little mustard seed that grows large with sturdy
branches and shade.
It's just a wee example of how our heart in faith grows, and our
place in heaven is made.

110. Do not judge one another, for that's surely not the way.
None of us are perfect, just one was perfect every day.

He sees with perfect eyes, He knows everything we know.
In others our eyes see flaws, yet miss the flaws of our own.
If you judge another, you will be judged just the same.
We are no greater than another, sin still leads us astray.
It is a part of this world, misleading us all along.
So turn to our Lord, to keep from doing wrong.
Do not judge another, since you are not the Christ.
Only He can judge each of us, then we will pay the price.
Try to look through eyes of love, see everyone in that way.
Quit looking for the wrong, instead, focus on the good every
    day.
Love your neighbor as yourself, like the Lord said we should.
If we don't quit judging one another, we will lose too much
    good.

111.   Worry not. Worry does not allow you to gain.
Worry not. Worry will not prevent pain.
Worry not. For with the Lord, needs are met.
Worry not. Worry does not dictate what we get.
Worry not. Unless you made no choice. Without the choice of
    Jesus, our soul has no voice.
Worry has no place, in a life led by our Lord.
Worry only brings more worry, so remember what you're told.
We must place our lives in God's hands.
We must trust He has the perfect plan.
So worry not, for it adds no time to your life.
So worry not, for with worry it only adds to strife.
Do not worry, Jesus will provide.
Do not worry, in Him you must abide.
Worry never solves any problems of man.
Turn worry to trust to see God's plan.

112.   Jesus chose twelve men, to teach and spread His word.
One man would betray Him, then another would be heard.
Their promise was to follow, yet much more would they give.
Some stumbled on their way but learned lessons how to live.

They grew the church Christ started, His mission for three years.
The path they continued, with persecution fears.
They never let that deter them, or even get in their way.
Jesus they followed, seeing death that fateful day.
They were visited when He arose from the grave.
The Son ascended to the Father, the Holy Spirit sent in His place.
The apostles now guided by the Spirit. Their connection to their savior remained.
Their work was the beginning of the church now sustained.
We can all be grateful for their work, telling why Jesus came.
Their mission is a light, a guide, so in Christ we can stay.
When you choose to follow Jesus, then your mission will begin.
Then continue the Lord's mission, telling others what Jesus did.

113. You bring love into our lives. You bring hope when we are discouraged.
You are company in our loneliness, never letting us feel forgotten.
You, Lord, chase us to bring us to You.
Undeserving, we fail on all levels. You do not quit the chase.
Your love always overflowing onto each of us.
We simply must accept that love and not shut You out.
Sadly some will miss Your call.
Some will deny Your love.
Some will merely walk alone, not knowing Your redemption.

114. To commune is to remain in close rapport.
The Lord always stays close to those reborn.
He asks us to remember Him, with a meal of bread and wine.
His flesh is the bread, His blood is the wine.
It is the way to honor Him, once we are reborn.
We need to always remember, the sacrifice He bore.

The act of communion, a simple act to show, as an act of
    remembrance for the story we must know.
It isn't just taking the bread and wine, but it's reevaluating
    what we are inside.
We must never forget His immeasurable love for us.
It's because of that love, life begins with Jesus.
We should pray each day, to know our Lord.
Know His word and follow, all that we are told.
The most precious gift given, the sacrifice was him.
Then when He arose from His death, salvation He did win.
A new life we can have, eternally to live.
Don't let this chance elude you, salvation He will give.
So whenever you take communion in His name, it's a simple
    act to honor the Savior that came.

115.   As we walk this world everyone is searching. Searching for
    fame, fortune, comfort, enjoyment, and success.
We can only be successful if we allow You, Lord, to be the light
    to success with redemption.
Only with You, will we find comfort in Your arms, fortune
    from Your word, fame through Your heart, and enjoy-
    ment doing Your work.
Open our eyes to see You as the end of our searching, the end
    of our struggles, the end of our failings, the end of a
    long and rocky road.
For it is in You, Lord Jesus, we will find our rest.

116.   Thank You, Lord, for finding me and not letting go.
Thank You for Your grace, as I continually fail You so.
Thank You for keeping me on Your path, even when I lose my
    way.
You guide me back to Your path, hoping I will stay.
I am grateful Your unchanging character anchors us in the
    storm.
It is a certainty in uncertain times, yet You find our faith is
    torn.

With so much chaos in the world, You, Lord, are the rock
    standing firm.
You are the gentle calming wave bringing calm to tumultuous
    seas, as life turns.
You alone are the peace in time of war, the respite in the chaos.
You, Lord Jesus, are the strength in weakness, the light in dark-
    ness, and the one to save us.
You are the safe haven in troubled times, and the love seen
    through the hate.
Help us Lord, to know this and help it grow our faith.
We can only find our way if we use You as our guiding light.
Ever faithful, forgiving, and just, You love us with such might.
Forever good, forever ours, if only we would ask.
Being patient with a broken world must be Your greatest task.

117.   Your miracles Lord eased the pain, gave sight to the blind, gave
    mobility to the crippled, and peace to the possessed.
You gave forgiveness, mercy, and compassion.
In You, Lord, the lost found righteousness, the righteous found
    humility, and the sinner found salvation.
Never would we be free without Your sacrifice.
Thank You for the love that goes beyond understanding.

118.   Obedience is Your request declared out of love.
Trust you ask, knowing with trust you give grace.
Truth is the word given reinforced by the Spirit.
Wisdom comes from You when we seek and ask.
Faith is a combination of obedience maintained,
Trust in your word, believing in its truth,
Sustained by the wisdom we gain when sought.
Faith becomes ours with belief that leads to salvation.
Obedience is our strength.

119.   My soul sings Your praise. My heart worships You, Lord. With
all my being I pour out gratitude for all You are, for all You
always have been, and for all we will see again. I await Your

arrival, yet am grateful for the time to convince others of the price You paid for us to be able to walk in Your light of salvation. Even when I long for You to bring me home, I am grateful for the time to tell Your story. Jesus, guide my words, my actions, and my heart to be reflective of Your light, Your joy, Your love, and Your open arms. Take me when You are ready, and when You do, I will forever praise the gift You died for. The gift of salvation that will light my way home. My way back to You.

120. I awake to the sun on a cold winter day.
Frost now where the snow had been.
It sparkles like twinkling stars as the sun shines on its crystals.
It is a reminder of the light You, Lord, brought to this world.
It is a reminder You are here still. Ever present in Your creation.
Ever present in the peace of a cold winter's day.
We praise You for the love and mercy You still pour out on a
      lost and broken world.
I praise You for opening my eyes to the gifts of Your creation.
I praise You for the gift of my salvation.
You do not have to be so good when we continue to disappoint.
But You are always good, even when You look at us with a
      broken heart, seeing so many broken people.
You still bring the sun, the frost, the warmth of Your love.
Faithful, gracious, and forgiving, Your character never waver-
      ing, never withheld.
In You I find peace. My praise to You, my Savior, Lord Jesus.

121. Do not think of evil things, or listen to what false teachers say.
Keep the Lord deep in your heart, keeping His word to guide
      your way.
Don't be like the Pharisees, making laws that shouldn't be.
Know the parables Christ told, so the best He will see.
It is a way for us to live, being kinder and gentler, learning
      how to give.

We praise You, Lord, for lessons learned, to help us teach others how to live.
Please search our hearts to let us know just how to learn and where to go.
Show us our hearts so we know who we are, let it guide us with love near and far.
For we are nothing if not focused on You.
We must be aware of what evil can do.
We will only be plagued with evil for so long, then Jesus will return correcting all wrong.
He will defeat evil and no more will it be.
Then the glory of God is all we will see.

122.   Have you been hurt by betrayal? Forgive.
Have you been injured by a cruel act? Forgive.
Have you had injustice in your life? Forgive.
Have you been forgotten and dismissed? Forgive.
Have you gone unseen due to race, creed, or poverty? Forgive.
Are you weary and overwhelmed? Ask.
Are you sorrowful and lost? Ask.
Are you hitting roadblock after roadblock? Ask.
Are you tired of illness and pain? Ask.
Do you find the world pressing in? Ask.
Are you lost in your sin? Ask.
Forgive by emulating the kindness and goodness of Jesus.
Forgive by calling on His name.
Ask for salvation freely given, taking your sins away.
Ask for guidance in your journey and God's peace in your life.
For the price paid, the character retained, the unconditional love we can call on our Lord, Jesus Christ.

123.   I prepare for my walk, Lord, in the night and in the light of day.
I praise You when the dew is on the flowers, and when dusk makes shadows go away.

You walk with me in the valley and on the mountain top never
    letting me lose my way.
Use me for Your glory each and every day.
You will find me anywhere my Lord, listening for what You
    say.
Teach me to tell others who You are and the reason that You
    came.
I wasn't much when You called my name, yet You pursued me
    all the same.
I walk closer now to the path You made.
I walk to honor You, Lord, for the price You paid.
You paid with Your life, Lord, You died suffering all our sins.
A pain we will never know or suffer because You, Lord, took
    away our sin.
I walk in the sun and in the cool of night.
I praise You in the walk and for Your eternal light.
I thank You for Your redemption and for Your light each day.
Thank You for the walk that guides me in Your way.

124.   Lord, why do people hate so openly? You see all with the loving eyes of the creator. Why do people hold resentment by categorizing groups of people for the attitudes of some? Lord Jesus, You see *each* person, not lumping people into groups.

Why do we oppose diversity so strongly? Did God create all flowers in one color, with one fragrance, or one texture? Does every animal have the same sound, same fur, feathers, or skin? Do the creatures of the sea all swim in the same pattern and same migration, or have the same instincts? Why do the mountains in the west not look like the mountains in the east? Jesus, You know the beauty of uniqueness. Some fields grow corn, some wheat, and some soybeans always being rotated. The earth supports them all. We see palm trees in the south, mighty oaks and firs in the north. Giant redwoods in the west and maple trees in the east all grow with much splendor.

Why can't we look at people through the eyes of the creator? We were made in God's image, yet each with our own unique identity. He did that with love. Our eyes, hair, and skin vary in shape, texture, and color. We aren't to be like cookies cut with the same cookie cutter, to be the same shape, size, flavor, and decoration. We are meant to be the best we can be as who we are.

Thank You, Lord, for the beauty in our individuality. Nothing should interfere with the path we are to take as well as the life we are each blessed to be given. We should try to enrich the lives of all around us with respect, encouragement, and inclusion. We should want for each other what we want for ourselves.

Our Lord found each and every one worth dying for. We all want to be loved, to be allowed to follow our dreams, and forge our own paths. No one should be judged too quickly, dismissed too readily, or not allowed to have a chance. You, Lord, are the judge not dismissing or ignoring.

Life is so much more joyful when lived without hate or judgment. Don't worry about what someone else has and what you don't. Our judgment at journey's end will not be dependent on what we have, but who we are. Quit thinking it is right to do what we want without regard for another. To be at peace with each other can bring more satisfaction than any dream realized.

We can choose better, love more, and embrace a life elevated by finding more room in our hearts for all created with God's loving hand. Jesus did not go to the cross to save a particular person. He went to save the individual He created to be with Him eternally. You, Lord, did it so we can all be in paradise with You. I am grateful for Your vast reaching love, mercy, forgiveness, and goodness. It is ever-present for each and every one. Jesus loves us as we are.

125.   Do you ever wonder why pain is allowed?
Why do we see the innocent suffer?
Why are children allowed to die?

Why do we continue to make poor choices allowing hate, prej-
    udice, and feelings of superiority to be our banner?
Why do we remain intent on controlling others for our gain?
Why do we allow any child, anywhere at any time to go
    hungry?
The price for our sin is the chaos we find in this world.
It is not put upon us but brought about by us.
We continue to live with greed, intolerance, selfishness, and
    unkindness.
All a byproduct of a broken world.
You, Lord Jesus, do not withhold compassion, love, forgive-
    ness, faithfulness, and mercy.
You, Lord, know each child You take back to Your loving arms.
Lord, bring comfort to those in pain.
Lord, open our eyes to the needy.
Only You, Lord, can guide us to be kinder, more selfless, more
    humble, more accepting of all and instill a giving heart.
With You, we can be forgiven and our sins washed away.
Only through You can we find salvation.
Only through you Lord, can we find the peace that goes
    beyond all human understanding.

126. Lord Jesus, You promise to return.
Your time is not our time, so patient in letting us learn.
Are we hearing Your warnings and learning what You want us
    to know?
Do we heed Your word, knowing You love us so?
So patient You are, watching as we continue to fail.
So patient You are, watching us struggle so faith will prevail.
Is it that one sheep You are seeking to bring home to You?
Many still take the wrong path, not knowing all that Your love
    can do.
I wonder, my Lord, each day that goes by, will there be time
    for those not hearing Your cry?
As they refuse Your path, I wonder if they see the futility of
    their ways.

Can You continue to watch as we all continue to stray?
Even those that love You, and I am one, failure
    still comes, though my heart You won.
I'm always being challenged with life so hard.
We see hate, abuse, neglect, and for You no regard.
If I struggle with the ways of this land, how much more pain-
    ful for You, who died sinless as a man?
I know when You are ready to put an end to this mess,
    Your timing will be perfect as we would expect no less.
From a perfect God to the one perfect man,
    You will wait for that lost sheep, as only You can.

127.   Walk beside us, Lord, lead us by the hand.
Keep us in Your sight, Lord, guide us in this land.
Help to keep us on Your path, not letting us lose our way.
Keep us in Your word, help us not to stray.
You are the only hope we have to survive this world we're in.
Your sacrifice gave us a chance to never die in sin.

128.   You allow suffering to make us whole.
You allow loss to draw us near.
You allow joy to nourish our soul.
You allow laughter for You to hear.
You give us love to bring us peace.
You give forgiveness when we believe.
You give comfort with pain released.
You give humility so conceit will cease.
My love to You for such things allowed.
My praise to You as Your giving abounds.

129.   We walk through valleys to reach mountains.
Never do You let us get lost in the depths or fall from the
    heights.
You shine light in the darkness and provide shade in the
    brightness.
You open doors to rooms where we hide.

You open windows for fresh air when we can't take a breath.
Ever present we are never forsaken, for Your love brought
    redemption.
We do not deserve such love You continually pour out.
I will praise You for such faithfulness, You consistently
    maintain.
I will praise You for the unfailing love, given in Your name.

130.   I see You in the ray of sun on a cloudy day.
I see You with the songbirds and when the chipmunks run
    and play.
I see You in the mighty oak, to the smallest apple tree.
I see You in the running brook, flowing to the sea.
You are in the fields of grain, and in the valleys lush and green.
You are the whisper in the wind and all that is unseen.
You are a part of Your creation, of earth, sea, and sky.
You, Lord Jesus, our strength and peace, as each moment
    passes by.

131.   You had family You loved and cared for, yet You walked this
    world seeing the Father's plan take form.
You denied Yourself the ways of man, remaining perfect in
    order to fulfill God's plan.
As man's evil continues to this day, they try to write stories that
    disregard Your way.
They can't believe You were devoid of sin so they tell stories
    that they imagine.
They won't believe You loved—without lust.
They appease their guilt due to lack of trust.
Are You certain we were meant to be saved?
How will we ever change our ways?
Even when we stumble and such depravity is seen.
You remain faithful, just waiting to redeem.

132.   Thank You for the miles You walked.
Thank You for the lessons taught.

Thank You for the tears You cried.
Thank You for Your actions so kind.
It was not easy the path You would take.
So much You would lose yet even more we would gain.
No matter what happened Your character remained.
We owe You so much, even more than we know.
We thank You, Lord, for the love You show.

133. Do you protect your heart from the world gone astray?
Do you guard your heart from the sins of each day?
Do you trust your heart to be faithful and true?
Do you control your heart when life comes at you?
This is not a task to be taken on alone.
This is not a path that easily leads home.
Our hearts, so precious, so tender, so weak, can only be
guarded when the Lord you seek.

134. The joy of a baby's laugh. The giggles that come when a puppy
licks a child's face.
A mother's sigh as her child is safe in bed at night.
A father's relief when he has provided for his family.
This occurs each day, even in this world.
The pain in the hungry child's cry. The sorrow as families
struggle to survive.
A mother's tears as she tries to keep her child warm.
A father's desperation called away to war.
This occurs each day, even in this world.
We know life will take many paths.
We also know in You, Jesus, we can rejoice, endure, and survive.

135. Do you know, you are loved today?
Do you know, you are why Jesus came?
Do you know, He knew we would fail?
Do you know, His love always prevails?
Know for you, the Lord's love is sustained.
Know for you, His forgiveness remains.

Know how much He wants you to believe.
Know He waits for your salvation received.

136.   The young man dies, yet a smile on his lips.
The parent cries giving up her child, yet You accept her praise
    for the two years they had.
The old man holds the hand of a wife who no longer knows
    him, yet he praises You for their many years together.
The woman leans over the only man that ever loved her,
    knowing he is gone. You, Lord, reassure her that he is
    with You.
The veteran struggles with visions of war and the pain of loss.
    You, Lord, put compassion, wisdom, and caring in his
    path.
The man lies in bed engulfed in burns from a heinous crime
    of racial prejudice. You, Lord, allowed him to forgive
    before he died.
The young man diagnosed with rare cancer. You, Lord, put the
    knowledgeable doctor in his path allowing his recovery.
The frightened woman struggles to breathe, not able to find
    comfort. You, Lord, showed her Your angel, bringing
    her peace.
A grieving family struggles with knowing they will lose the
    one they love. You, Lord, showed them how to celebrate
    his life.
A daughter giving up the mother that sustained her faith,
    always comforted her, and greatly loved her family. You,
    Lord, gave the daughter the father to care for.
All these things I have seen or lived, Lord, and you always
    showed me You were present in the moment.
I praise You for comfort given, love sustained, forgiveness
    encouraged, and for showing me we are never out of
    Your sight or Your reach.

137. John, Peter, and Paul sacrificed much once receiving the call.
John was persecuted, yet his life spared, he wrote Christ's story to be shared.
Peter preached God's Word of salvation, his faith caused his crucifixion.
Paul a persecutor of believing Jews was converted then spread the good news.
These three men changed mankind. From them, salvation many would find.
Their legacies long reaching through time, God's Word now on our minds.
We don't need to be famous like them, just share God's Word and worship Him.
So many sacrificed their lives for the Lord, just so Christ's story could be told.
Still today, for faith many die because the world embraces a lie.
Just remember the high price you'll pay, if you don't follow the Lord's way.
So thank the men who showed the way, in our hearts they will stay.
Remembered for the truth they spoke, and for the words they later wrote.
They continue to live on in the truth they wrote, repeating the words Jesus spoke.
So important to hear the Word of our Lord, death could not stop the truth from being told.

138. Forgiving, faithful, good, just, kind, truthful and loving.
All in Your character, Lord Jesus, all poured out on us, though we are not worthy.
You never deny us the benefit of Your character.
We forget how faithful You remain in our struggle.
We become frustrated thinking we don't see justice.
Your justice not always in our time but always in Yours.
The truth You give us, yet we often deny it.
Kindness and love we always see in You, then and now.

Your goodness, never failing, goes beyond our comprehension.
Your forgiveness is a gift for accepting who You are and sacri-
fice given.
Help us gain Your character in our walk with You.
Help us know Your character, to accept in our lives.

139.   Joy comes from Your love and grace.
Joy comes when finding our place.
Joy comes each morning given.
Joy comes with song raised to heaven.
Joy comes from knowing You.
Joy comes from all You do.
Joy, You brought to all mankind, with belief, redemption we
will find.

140.   Your word, Lord, so often misconstrued.
Man uses it to bring himself comfort yet not follow You.
You tell us not to judge, lest we be judged, yet we use Your
word to condemn those that do not follow, those that
are not loved.
We can love those that have strayed from Your path.
No single soul, only You have ever made perfection last.
Preaching alone won't bring anyone to You.
Once told who You are You draw them to You.
You loved the sinners, You forgave their ways.
You healed the sick, loved the unloved, and for this You paid.
We won't die the death You suffered for us.
Once it was done, we in salvation could trust.
So why can't we walk beside those You have embraced?
Dear Lord, help us, so with You much pain can be erased.

141.   I sing Your praise and worship Your name.
I read Your word, and Your guidance came.
Insight and wisdom, I pray You will bring.
Your hand on all children, no matter their needs.
Your peace for the elderly, as their journey nears end.

Your guidance for the young, for they question how to begin.
For those in mid-journey, Your faithfulness they need.
In this broken, chaotic world, Your goodness must be seen.
Only with You, can we find our way.
You, Lord Jesus, in our hearts please stay.

142. You broke down barriers, You sought the lost.
You taught new lessons, all knowing the cost.
You looked at the world, in a different light.
You wanted us to see, the world through Your sight.
Injustice at times was met with Your wrath.
Yet kindness and compassion, primarily Your path.
We know You wept, at the loss of a friend
        even when knowing his life would not end.
You honored the Father, with the timing asked.
Knowing this miracle had a greater task.
It had to be seen, at just the right time.
It had to be seen, by just the right kind.
To merely bring Lazarus back from the dead,
        wasn't as important as what would be said.
For those that believed, this news would have might, so many
        Jews converted on sight.
Jesus knew, His time to leave was drawing near.
He led His disciples in absence of fear.
He needed His disciples to witness what He would do.
Time short, much left to teach before He was through.

143. My heart is heavy when I think of the price You paid.
My heart is grateful for those that paved the way.
Much suffering occurred to make certain the world knew.
Your sacrifice paid for redemption, leading to You.
I am joyful in the salvation Your suffering brought.
I am grateful for the lessons You taught.
I find hope in knowing mankind has been given this chance.
With our belief, our life will be enhanced.
Salvation can only come if we believe in Your story.

No greater gift can there be than to be with You in Glory.

144. Our doubts, our insecurities, fueled by a world of chaos and
struggle.
Our regrets, our wandering path, lack of faith, humility gone.
Our prayers unanswered, dreams dashed, we don't trust in
Your infinite wisdom.
Our sorrows, our grief, a dark pit where we block Your light
and don't listen to Your voice.
I will most likely remain insecure, but I feel Your reassurance
in the value You give me.
I had regrets, knowing I strayed from the path charted for me,
yet You forgave.
I am growing in faith, knowing I do not always need to know
why Your choices may not be mine.
Some prayers are not to be answered.
You know our wants are not always our needs.
I will continue to have sorrow but not in dark or deep despair.
My sorrow comes when others deny Your presence and how
much You care.
You bring me peace when I am grieved.
The grief I feel comes from knowing there are those that will
remain lost.
You, Jesus, died so we could be free of sin and safe in Your
loving care.
You then rose to reassure us prophecy was fulfilled and salva-
tion won.
The salvation offered, freely given, this is the message we must
share.

145. Our doubts You replace with reassurance. Our fears You
replace with resolve.
Our disappointment You replace with hope. Our confusion
You turn to clarity.
Our weakness You turn into strength. When we stumble You,
Lord, pick us up.

When in pain You bring comfort. Because of Your love, when
lost You find us.
When drowning in sin, You paid the price for our redemption.
You, Jesus, gave us life when we were dead. You brought light
to the darkness.

146. Your life for pieces of silver, betrayed by one You loved. Yet
You were willing, knowing the cost.
Beaten, humiliated, defiled, Your clothes divided by the roll of
the dice. Yet You were willing, knowing the cost.
Pierced by a sword, mocked, and jeered, our King, our Lord,
our Savior treated worse than a criminal. Yet You were
willing, knowing the cost.
You were separated from the Father, the sins of man crushing
You. Yet You were willing, knowing the cost.
We the recipients of Your willingness, now found no longer
lost.

147. So weary, Lord, I am weary with the only strength remaining
from You alone.
Nothing on the earth can restore my strength.
Nothing on the earth can restore my tired soul.
You, Lord, are the light that continues to shine in the darkness.
You, Lord, bring rest to the weary and hope to the hopeless.
You, Lord, bring peace to hearts devastated by warring nations.
You, Lord, are company in our loneliness.
Your faithfulness sustains us. Your goodness encourages us.
Your justice restores our hope. Your forgiveness renews our soul.
Only Your love can redeem, fulfill, and strengthen the weary soul.

148. Jesus, thank You for loving each one of us and offering salvation to anyone who believes. You do not deny any of us,
no matter our circumstances, no matter our appearance. You
created us all, and see beauty in every one of us. Help us to see
each other through Your eyes. Help us to see the worth of each

individual as You do. We praise You for the diversity seen, the
diversity needed, and the reward of loving amidst the diversity.
You, Lord, see our beauty, our potential, and our individuality.
I am grateful, Lord, Your love is greater than our intolerance.

149. Lord Jesus, You taught in parables.
Stories imparting lessons along the way.
You taught Your disciples as You walked.
By example, they learned what to say.
You performed miracles, forgave the sinner, and sent demons
        out and away.
You restored life to the lifeless, Your compassion showed no
        bounds.
You gave a new covenant, a new way of living to be found.
No longer tied to endless laws that so many could no longer
        maintain.
You did not disregard the teachings of the past, giving laws all
        could sustain.
Only two, should be easy, from the Father who sent us these
        laws.
So simple in context, so clearly stated, easily understood by all.
Then why has it been so difficult, for man to master this sim-
        ple task?
You made it so easy to change our path, so little did You ask.
"Putting God above all else," for our creation and salvation, we
        should be honored for this task.
Yet in a world so tempting in its sin, we constantly turn our
        back.
"To love your neighbor as yourself," the rewards endless when
        we follow that path.
Yet again, we lean into the voices of hate, with love of self a
        lesser task.
I don't know what it will take, dear Lord, for these two simple
        laws to be kept.
Why can we not see how misguided we are, how our path
        becomes inept?

Praise and love, You were the master at both, when You walked
on earth as a man.
Your love remained, Your covenant given, Your sacrifice put
salvation at hand.
How much more as such fragile beings, in a world so torn
apart, could we ever ask our Creator, our God, when He
freely gave us His heart.

150. Jesus, You are the light of the world, the Good Shepherd, the
King of kings.
You, dear Jesus, are the Prince of Peace, the Savior, the one
who rights all things.
Son of God, Son of Man, You are all to everyone.
You were part of creation as the Trinity, You were more than
just the Son.
Called by so many names that tell us who You are.
Emmanuel, God with us, explains Your near not far.
It matters not what name Your given, to each Your blessing is
clear.
You are our Redeemer, our friend, and the teacher we all must
hear.
It's necessary we know Your name, for belief is all we need.
We simply must call the name of Jesus, so we may be redeemed.

151. Guard my heart, Lord, keeping out malice, evil, and anger.
Guard my words, Lord, keeping them kind, loving, and
truthful.
Guard my actions, Lord, keeping them honorable, loyal, and
focused on service.
You, Lord Jesus, gave us hope through Your character and
example.
Your heart pure and free of sin.
Your words give us purpose, guidance, and insight as to what
we must be.
Your actions of service, patience, and mercy gave us the exam-
ple to emulate.

From You, salvation given freely if we just believe.

152. Jesus, You ask so little, only for the love of our creator and savior.
Jesus, You ask so little, to love our fellow man as we love ourselves.
Jesus, You ask so little, so simple in its instruction and intent.
Jesus, You ask so little, creating us and giving us all our needs.
Jesus, You ask so little, creating us in likeness and character, yet we don't recognize it in each other or self.
Jesus, You ask so little, for our simple belief and love with Your guidance.
Jesus, You ask so little, when there was nothing little about Your task.
Jesus, make us little to self, great to trust in Your word.
Jesus, we did not ask, yet You gave it all, for our redemption.

153. Praise, worship, obedience, all I give to You.
Love, service, compassion, all I give for You.
Forgiveness, patience, kindness, all I give because of You.
Peace, salvation, eternity, all I have from You.

154. No other place would I rather be than in the arms, of the one who saved me.
No other one do I want to see than the Lord and Savior that guides me.
No other time do I want it to be than when it's time for my Lord to see.

155. To the little children, He said come.
To the parents, "Bring your daughter and your son."
He gathered each child close to Him.
Loving each, knowing He would die for them.
To everyone else He gave a lesson to hear.
To receive God's kingdom as a child, so He can draw you near.

For if you don't see Him through their eyes, to you His king-
    dom will be denied.
For the wonder seen through a child's eyes, is to our Lord, no
    question or surprise.
He puts it there, to give them a good start.
He prays when we grow, we'll keep it in our heart.
Do not be cynical, hardened, or vain.
Keep your childlike eyes, and in Christ remain.

156.   He walked a sinless path teaching as He went.
No one too poor, too sick, too sinful, for His time spent.
His disciples, learning each day they had with Him.
Some more faithful than others, at time their faith dim.
He knew each one's path, He knew what each would sacrifice.
His choices for His church, for His glory, for our lives.
His love endless, His goodness unexpected, His mission,
    self-sacrificing.
All for the world, for mankind, all for redirecting.
Never before seen such a cost, to bring us out of eternal loss.
Never again would this price be paid.
For once it was done, salvation came.

157.   Mary and Joseph, parents so loving, so faithful, so good.
They knew who You were, trusting God, doing all they could.
The carpenter taught You to use Your hands.
Your mother taught you the lessons God planned.
Two mortal people, so brave, so true. They knew what their
    son had to do.

158.   Your parables, stories with lessons told.
A way of teaching in days of old.
So much wisdom and knowledge You did impart.
You did it all to change our heart.
The parable of the seed, landing on different ground.
Telling us how Your word is heard, and how its meaning is
    found.

You tell of how sometimes it takes root, yet also can fade away.
The soil sometimes accepts the seed, yet often a strong root
     not made.
You tell us the story of the weeds in wheat, the wheat is good,
     the weeds are not.
You caution not to pull the weeds, or the wheat may also come
     loose from the plot.
When You reap Your harvest You will separate weed from
     wheat.
The wheat will remain with You, yet the weed You will not
     receive.
The parable of the yeast, so small when in the flour to start.
It grows the dough to great size, it's in the bread's every part.
Your kingdom small like the grains of yeast, would grow to
     great size from the *least of these*.
These tales of how faith and Your kingdom grows, expresses
     how it's You we all must know.
So many parables overtime were told.
Your wisdom in stories would steadily unfold.
Each parable we must take to heart.
Each one has wisdom, His love to impart.

159.   All sin is offensive to God. Lies are as abhorrent to God as someone not following His law. Evil is evil and that we all recognize. Do not mistake all choices as evil if they offend your sensibilities. Love rather than judge, choose peace over confrontation, and understanding over disregard. Jesus knows the heart of each person and the intent of each one of our thoughts. Don't miss out on being the one to bring a smile to the one ignored, comfort to the one disregarded and acceptance to the one shunned.

Our love can be more powerful than another's sin. We aren't the one to do the judging. Leave sin for Jesus to judge. Work on correcting your own sin. Work on loving more each day to grow your heart. Be reflective of the light of Christ. Not everyone knows Him. Let them see Him in us, by the love we express. Only you, Lord, can help us walk a more faithful path, and to live a life choosing love over judgement. You alone are our strength in the journey.

160. We all have known sorrow, we all have known joy.
We all have known pain, we all had hearts broken before.
To some, it has been to a lesser degree.
To some, it overwhelms, and they question how to be free?
When you read God's word you will discover Jesus experienced all of this.
He wept with friends Martha and Mary and Joseph he must have missed.
We could hear the joy in His words when He gathered little children close to Him.
There was joy, in the fellowship shared with disciples, and when the hearts of people He would win.
We know He felt pain in the garden as He knew what was to come.
We could feel His heart broken by disciples, sleeping not supporting the One.
We could guess His heart broke even though He knew betrayal would come.
Yet even worse, when the betrayer didn't ask forgiveness for what he had done.
His pain, not to a lesser degree, nothing would be easy for our Lord, in the body of a man.
As flesh was torn to the bone, as spikes were driven through His hands.
Pain came with the separation from His Father as He took on our sins.
His humiliation from His naked body and from all the mocking given Him.
Unbearable it all would be to any person alive.
What we think we can't endure, He already had, and then He died.

His divinity won over His humanity knowing what had to be
    done.
Our God, the Holy Trinity separated to assure mankind had
    won.
If it wasn't for the miracle that followed on that third day.
All of our pain and suffering would never be taken away.

161.   I want to be among the people that drew near to You.
Thousands gathered within Your sight learning all You could
    do.
You told of the kingdom that awaits each of us.
You told how to love, and how belief is a must.
You are the Son of God, they saw Your glory.
They heard who You are, told in each story.
We can't sit on a mountain to listen to You.
But You left Your word, telling what we can do.
Such a blessing we were never left behind.
You tell us each, how salvation we can find.

162.   I sit in solitude, reflecting on all that You are.
I write of Your love, and Your redemption spread far.
I pray for Your guidance, so no one is misled.
My heart full of love, for all that You said.
For each person I want this same peace.
You gave it all, Your soul released.
I want so badly for this world to come to You.
I want so badly for them to know Your truth.
With each word written, You guided my pen.
With each word heard, a life can begin.
My precious Lord Jesus, let more people hear.
Of Your unending love that overpowers fear.
My life would be lost, if You weren't by my side.
You give me so much, You healed my mind.
Please let my words impart Your wisdom and love.
Please let people know You are here, as well as above.
To reach You is so simple a task.

They must believe and do what You ask.

163. My disobedience, my selfishness, my frustration with my
      enemy, my lack of trust,
      All sins, all needing correction with Your guidance.
      All for which I seek Your forgiveness.
      All You already knew and already forgave.
      All covered by redemption given for belief in Your name.

164. You prepare our place. You long for us to be with You.
      You told us that eternity is not in this world.
      You gave it all to have us with You.
      We must prepare our hearts for eternity.
      We must know and accept that this world is not our home.
      We must give You all our heart and obedience to be with You.

165. You chose the lowly shepherd boys to be first to tell of Your
            arrival.
      You chose humble surroundings rather than a palace for Your
            birth.
      You chose ordinary men to follow You.
      You chose to eat with sinners rather than royalty.
      You chose to elevate the position of women and children.
      You chose the lost, the sick, the lame, the possessed to come
            to You.
      You chose suffering, humiliation, and injustice to be Your fate.
      You chose a broken world, to love and redeem.
      You chose the least of these.
      You chose me.

166. The narrow gate and narrow path is how we get to You.
      The wide gate only leads to our destruction.
      Your path is ours to follow, narrow and straight, while waiting
            to enter the gate.
      Don't let us swing wide, not returning to the path You made
            for us.

Don't let us lose focus on our goal to reach the narrow gate.
Let us see You at the end of the narrow path.
Let us avoid the wide path of this world that does not allow us
    sight of You.
Open our hearts to You that will allow the narrow gate to open.
Don't let it shut, only leaving the option of our destruction
    down the wide path.
In You, we are given the option to follow or to dismiss.
Thank You for leading my heart to follow You down that nar-
    row path.
My love for You will open the narrow gate.
My devotion to You will allow me to be in Your presence.
No greater gift will there ever be.

167. I hold the hand pierced by the nail.
I follow the steps of the feet scarred by the spike.
My thirst, satisfied with fresh spring water, not vinegar.
My breath easy, lungs not filled with water.
My blood, cleansed by Yours. My sins You left behind.
My death fleeting, the grave not claiming me.
My life You gave me, redeemed by Your blood.
Eternity now a reality, not a goal unreachable due to my sin.
Your unconditional love realized because of Your sacrifice.

168. You are the wise man. You are the shepherd.
You are the bright shining star.
You are the humility of a humble birth.
You are the sinless baby, remaining sinless as a man.
You are the hope, the way, the truth, and the life.
Lead us to You.

169. Bright was the star that shone for You.
Brighter still, the light You brought into the world.
Dark was the sin we were lost in.
Dark was the path we were following.
New was the covenant You brought.

New was the salvation You would give.
Old was the law man failed to follow.
Old was the hopelessness being felt by so many.
You are the guiding star, the light, for all.
You find the lost, brighten our path and give us Your word.
The new covenant given. Salvation, hope, and guidance, ours
    for the asking.
Our path is now bright with glory within our reach.
Your word, our guide, our affirmation.
You came to give this world another chance.
A chance to change and accept salvation.
We can now be whole in Your love and redemption.
We can now be whole in a relationship with You.

170. Lord Jesus, You are the answer to all questions.
Only You know our future as we continue in sin.
Only You know why war continues and suffering doesn't cease.
Only You know the hour You will remove the evil one's reign.
It is that promise that gives me comfort in this suffering world.
Your promise sustains hope and allows joy.
You bring peace to the troubled heart.
Let every person find hope in Your faithfulness.
Encourage us all to accept Your unfailing love.

Conclusion

These are not like the Psalms of the Old Testament. My writing style is rather unorthodox, and it is focused on Jesus and His influence. No matter the writing style, I hope you gain something from the content.

Much was written regarding the sacrifice Jesus made. That is because it is the one greatest thing ever done for all mankind since creation.

All were written with the greatest love and respect for the most important person in my life. My prayer is that it will encourage you to seek a relationship with Jesus, or deepen the one you have already established. There is much repetition. I hope if it does not touch you when stated one way that it will reach you when stated differently. Thank you for indulging me and reading my work.

About the Author

Beth Marie Hawley retired after thirty years as a critical care registered nurse. She had to give up her professional career as an RN early due to lupus of the brain and central nervous system. It was her honor to continue to care for family and friends as God called her to do. Due to her lupus, she could no longer read conventional writing. The Bible was all she could continue to read for the next seventeen years. She recovered from lupus after seventeen years. This is not the known outcome of lupus. It was after that healing, she felt a strong calling to write Bible studies and devotional books. Her love of Christ Jesus is what sustained her through triumph and tragedy. Her goal in writing this book was to introduce people to the love of Christ. For those that know Him, she hopes they will have a greater appreciation of Jesus after reading this.

Beth is devoted to following her Lord's guidance. She is blessed with two remarkable adult children. Her beloved husband of fifteen years, Bob, returned to the Lord over twenty years ago. He honorably served the United States for thirty years in the US Navy. She has remained a widow since his passing. Her family and church family bring her much joy and satisfaction. It is her faith that brings her peace.